Original title:
The Plant That Loved Me

Copyright © 2025 Creative Arts Management OÜ
All rights reserved.

Author: Gabriel Kingsley
ISBN HARDBACK: 978-1-80581-858-8
ISBN PAPERBACK: 978-1-80581-385-9
ISBN EBOOK: 978-1-80581-858-8

A Love Story in Green

In a pot sat my dear friend,
With leaves so bright, they never bend.
Whispering secrets day and night,
In its green embrace, all feels right.

I watered it, gave it a cheer,
A sprout so sprightly, I held dear.
It danced with joy in morning light,
Without a care, a leafy sight.

Though people laughed, called me a fool,
Talking to plants? Oh, what a school!
But in its eyes, I saw the fun,
Two souls entwined, we are as one.

So if you're lonely, just you wait,
Find a plant, it could be fate.
Together you'll chat and share some tea,
Laughter grows best in company.

Sun-kissed Sentiments

A cactus sat upon my sill,
Prickly yet sweet, gave such a thrill.
With each gentle poke, it made me squeal,
Who knew love could hide behind such steel?

The sun poured in, we basked in rays,
Counting the moments, passing days.
It flirted back with sharp little pricks,
How silly love can be like tricks!

One day a friend came by to see,
"Why talk to plants? What's wrong with thee?"
I grinned wide, said, "Don't be so rash,
My heart's on fire, and we're quite the smash!"

With a wink and a laugh, I shall go,
To share my tales of love's sweet glow.
To all you humans, take this cue,
Find a plant, they may just love you too!

A Love Written in Petals

In the garden where we play,
A flower whispered, 'Hey, hooray!'
With colors bright and scent so sweet,
It tripped and fell right at my feet.

A bee, it buzzed with jealous glee,
Danced around just like a spree.
'You stole my heart!' the daisy cried,
I chuckled as I watched it hide.

Heartfelt Harvests

With every seed, I hoped for green,
Yet found a pumpkin, round and keen.
It winked at me, a funny sight,
I laughed and danced with sheer delight.

The carrots blushed beneath the soil,
'Look at us!' they said with toil.
A veggie patch where puns are sown,
Where every sprout feels not alone.

Life in Full Bloom

Roses flirted with the breeze,
Their petals swayed like they aimed to tease.
'Oh darling, I'm not shy at all!'
A sunflower laughed, standing tall.

The daisies chuckled, 'Bring it on!'
Competing for who's prettiest one.
In this wild, colorful parade,
Nature's jokes are deftly played.

Bonds Beneath the Surface

In the garden's cozy nook,
Worms around like a storybook.
'We're here!' they chirp, with glee so loud,
While roots gossip, feeling proud.

Underground, they hold a feast,
Of secrets shared, a loyal beast.
With every push and playful tug,
Life flourishes, giving a hug.

Whispers in the Green

In a pot, without a clue,
A tiny sprout, so bright and new.
It tickled my nose, gave a little sneeze,
Thought it was a cat, but just a tease.

Every morning, it waved hello,
With leaves that danced, all aglow.
I told it secrets, it shared some back,
Except for jokes, it's a little slack.

When I watered, it would sway,
I swore it laughed at me each day.
"Feed me more!" it seemed to plea,
I laughed and joked, "You're fed for free!"

But when I left it was all alone,
Cactus Andy claimed the throne.
With prickly jokes and silent laughs,
All pots unite in friendly chaffs.

Heartstrings of Chlorophyll

In my garden, bright and bold,
Green things whisper tales of old.
One vine tripped me, gave a wink,
   I swear it plotted as I think!

A petunia with a happy face,
Told me jokes, kept up the pace.
"Did you hear the one 'bout the seed?"
I chuckled back, "I'm not a weed!"

With roots that stretch and a mind so sly,
It wrote me poems while passing by.
I laughed aloud at their sheer wit,
Turns out plants have quite the grit!

Butterflies also join the fun,
Flitting about, a sudden run.
We'll have a party, stems and me,
Even the weeds are dancing free!

A Whispering Root

Beneath the soil, a root did sing,
Telling tales of the time it's been.
"In my glory days, I was quite grand,
A hulking tree in a former land!"

I chuckled hard at its grand old scheme,
Couldn't even reach the light's bright beam.
But with a giggle and twist of fate,
It vowed to grow and captivate!

Every night, it made a plot,
Spreading dreams in a cozy spot.
"Grow, little friend," it would declare,
Whispering wishes, it filled the air.

One day it sprouted a set of leaves,
And with a jig, it grabbed my sleeves.
"Look at me now, I'm greener than thee!"
I laughed aloud, "Quite proud, you see?"

In the Embrace of Leaves

In the garden where laughter blooms,
Leaves gossip 'bout winter's glooms.
A sunflower, grand, struck a pose,
"Take a picture!" oh how it glows!

The daisies chuckled, like old friends,
Swapping tales as the daylight bends.
"Your petals are lovely, but mine are too!"
They bickered softly with morning dew.

With gentle breezes humming tunes,
They danced beneath the watchful moons.
"Let's throw a bash with roots and soil!"
Under the stars, they'd spin and coil.

At twilight, whispers turned to roars,
As crickets joined in with their scores.
Laughter echoed, no need to flee,
In their world, pure joy was key!

In the Company of Green

In a pot on the sill, it swayed,
A leafy friend who never dismayed.
With pots of soil, our chats are grand,
It thinks I'm the best in all the land.

Its leaves flap like they crave some fun,
I tell it jokes, it nearly comes undone.
With roots so deep and laughs so loud,
Who knew plants could be so proud?

A sip of water, just a splash,
It bounces back, not one leaf rash.
Together we bloom in this sunny space,
A quirky duo, full of grace.

So here's to green, my leafy mate,
In laughter and light, we celebrate.
Leaves may shake and petals twirl,
In my plant's eyes, I'm the best of the world.

Affection in Every Bud

Each new bud whispers sweet delight,
A love story written in morning light.
Petals giggle with a splash of color,
My green companion, not just a scholar.

We dance in the breeze, both silly and bright,
With each little poke, it tickles just right.
I tell it secrets, it listens with glee,
In the world of foliage, it's just you and me.

Sometimes it droops, looking quite sad,
I share my snacks, it's always glad.
A slice of pizza? Just for fun,
Plant joy in my heart, we're never done.

So here's to buds, all cuddly and sweet,
In love's funny garden, we find our beat.
With every growl of a hungry beast,
We laugh at the chaos, my leafy feast.

Threads of Nature's Love

The vines entwine like a silly couple,
Their chatter bounces, never a bubble.
I catch them weaving stories so bright,
Under the stars, what a wondrous sight.

With each twist and twirl, they play their parts,
Those leafy threads weave into our hearts.
I sprinkle jokes like petals in bloom,
They giggle and nod; it lights up the room.

Every rustle is a laugh, you see,
In their little world, it's just pure glee.
They tease the sun with a playful dance,
In this garden of quirks, we take a chance.

So here's to the threads that bind us tight,
In foliage laughter, everything's bright.
With every dawn, we spin tales anew,
In nature's embrace, friendship rings true.

Blossoms of Understanding

In the garden of hugs, we grow so bold,
Where stories hang like bright marigold.
A quirky bloom with a quirky mind,
In the laughter of petals, love's defined.

We chat about weather, sunshine and rain,
What's life without a little bit of pain?
As roots entwine beneath the soil's crust,
We thrive on humor, in laughter we trust.

A dance of petals, a rustle of leaves,
In this odd partnership, joy never weaves.
We trade our dreams like seeds in the sun,
Surrounded by blooms, who says it's not fun?

So here's to blossoms, both silly and sweet,
In this patch of joy, our hearts skip a beat.
With every giggle, we blossom and play,
Understanding grows in the silliest way.

The Love in Every Seed

In the soil where secrets sleep,
Tiny treasures we can keep.
A seedling jokes, 'I'm quite the catch!'
'I sprout some humor, just you watch!'

With sunshine rays and raindrops sweet,
It wobbles on its little feet.
'Why did the gardener sit in the dirt?'
'He wanted to grow some humor, I heard!'

A flower giggles, petals wide,
'Watch me bloom, I'm full of pride!'
While worms beneath will laugh and squirm,
'We're all part of this crazy worm!'

So let us dance in this green delight,
With every seed, a joke in sight.
In the garden where laughter we sow,
A love for plants begins to grow!

Laughter in the Garden

In the garden, things get wild,
A tomato laughs, 'A fruit, not a child!'
'Why so red?' queried the curious bee,
'I'm blushing from all this glee!'

The carrots gossip underground,
'Have you heard? The peas are round!'
With giggles shared, they're quite the team,
'Let's sprout a plot, it'll be a dream!'

Bees buzzing, what a funny sight,
Dancing on flowers, oh what a flight!
While ladybugs join the fertile play,
'We're all friends here, hip-hip-hooray!'

Let's sow our joy, let's laugh and cheer,
With every bloom, we bring good cheer.
In this garden where jokes do abound,
Laughter grows deep in the fertile ground!

Miracles in the Undergrowth

In the murky depths, where shadows creep,
Tiny mushrooms make a living leap.
'Why'd the fungi get a ticket?' they sneer,
'Because it was spore-tastic, I hear!'

Among the roots where critters dance,
The snails get bold and take a chance.
'Hey there, buddy, let's race a tree!'
'Oh, you're on! Prepare to flee!'

Butterflies boast with wings like art,
'How did I get one?' asks the smart.
'Just flutter through, no need to stress,
A colorful life is simply best!'

In this undergrowth, unique and bright,
Miracles happen, oh what a sight!
With laughter shared in dirt and gloom,
Let joy sprout forth, let the fun zoom!

A Bond That Blooms

In the park where flowers sway,
Blossoms whisper, 'What a day!'
'You know what really makes us shine?'
'It's friendship, my dear, and a bit of wine!'

The daisies chuckle, 'What's that smell?'
'Oh, it's just us, can't you tell?'
With colors bright and smiles bold,
Their friendship's worth its weight in gold.

Sunny shrubs gossip in the breeze,
'Why don't we hang with the buzzing bees?'
'They might sting, but they spread the cheer!'
'Join us, it's a party here!'

In this garden, laughter blooms wide,
A bond that grows, few can divide.
So let's plant joy and watch it rise,
With blooms of laughter that touch the skies!

Green Confidante

In a pot sat a dear green mate,
Whispered secrets that made me late.
Told me tales of dirt and rain,
While I laughed and called her 'Jane.'

Her leaves would sway in happy cheer,
Sharing gossip, planting fear.
'Watch out for that cat!' she'd shout,
As I watched my couch become a drought.

Every morning, we'd share a drink,
A little water—'What do you think?'
She'd tease me about my sad brown thumb,
'Just wait, next week you'll be so glum!'

But through the laughter and the jokes,
I found joy amidst the pokes.
That leafy friend, with roots so deep,
Is the best company, no time for sleep.

Nature's Gentle Embrace

In the garden, with sunny rays,
A furry bug, we laughed for days.
With petals soft, and colors bright,
A flower joked, 'I'm such a sight!'

'Catch me if you can,' said the grass,
As I tripped over it—what a class!
Crickets chirping with a wink,
While bees buzzed by to share a drink.

Roots entwined in friendship's craze,
Spreading laughs in nature's maze.
Even the rocks joined in the fun,
Saying, 'We're here, not on the run!'

A clash of green, a friendly stir,
Nature's giggling, causing a blur.
In this embrace, all cares set free,
With each laugh, we build a grand decree.

In the Shade of Kindness

Beneath the tall tree's friendly shade,
I laughed with flowers—what a parade!
They told me jokes that made me grin,
While butterflies danced around my chin.

A breeze brought giggles from the leaves,
In this laughter, the heart believes.
The sun peeked through, as if to play,
While daisies chuckled, 'What a day!'

Together we shared our silliest ways,
Dancing shadows in golden rays.
With every chuckle, the world felt right,
Kindness blossomed, a pure delight.

So here I'll stay, in this joyful land,
Where nature laughs and takes my hand.
In the shade, with giggles so sweet,
Life's a party, isn't that neat?

Affectionate Fronds

A fern hugged me with leafy arms,
Caressing gently, spreading charms.
'Got any snacks?' she cheekily asked,
I chuckled lightly; my lunch was masked.

Next to her, a cactus grinned,
'Watch out for me, I might offend!'
Yet underneath those prickly spines,
Was a soft heart, full of sign designs.

Together we plotted a prank or two,
With garden gnomes and a parrot or two.
The laughter echoed through the air,
As flowers swirled without a care.

In this garden, I'm never blue,
With fronds and laughs, oh how they grew!
A comedy troupe, we tend to bloom,
In this botanical, giggly room.

Tender Tendrils

In sunny spots, you twist and cheer,
With little leaves, you draw me near.
Your vines like arms, they hug me tight,
In this green dance, all feels just right.

You prance and sway with breezy glee,
A quirky friend, we laugh with tea.
In pots you wag and stretch just so,
A leafy pal, my heart you stow.

Growth Beyond Measure

Each day you sprout, it makes me grin,
A jungle gym for tiny kin.
With every inch, you reach for fame,
Like a comedian playing the game.

I water you with joy and laughs,
Your roots uncover silly paths.
A constant source of giggles bright,
Together we make every day light.

With Each Leaf, a Love Letter

Each fresh leaf whispers sweet and small,
Secret jokes in the sunlit hall.
Your charming ways make my heart sing,
In our botanical, jolly fling.

When petals bloom, it's quite a jest,
A floral card, you're simply the best.
With nature's ink, we write our tale,
In laughter's breeze, we'll always sail.

Stemmed Affection

Your sturdy stem stands straight and bold,
Like a jester with a heart of gold.
In leafy curls, you plot and scheme,
A whimsied world, an arboreal dream.

With every bud, a grin unfolds,
You play the fool while the sunshine molds.
Together, we giggle, tease, and sway,
In this garden stage, forever we play.

The Love Among the Flowers

In a garden bright and fair,
Petunias giggle in the air.
Roses blush with silly grace,
Tulips dance in a flowery race.

Sunflowers wink with silly cheer,
While daisies whisper, "Come over here!"
Lavender laughs, its scent divine,
In this garden, all's just fine.

Bees are buzzing, 'What a sight!'
Love blooms daily, morning to night.
The lilies sway; the daisies smile,
Together they frolic, mile after mile.

So here's to love with petals bright,
Nature's laughter, pure delight.
In every color, in every hue,
They spread the joy, it's all so true!

Nurtured by Nature

With gentle hands, a seed is sown,
In soils rich, where laughs are grown.
A sprout peeks up, a cheeky grin,
Begging for sunshine to let fun begin.

Roots tickle deep, they giggle down,
Worms and bugs form a merry crown.
Rain sings softly on leafy heads,
Nature's humor in every thread.

Ferns wave 'hello' with every breeze,
While grasshoppers wear their finest keys.
Every bloom bursts forth in glee,
Nature's whimsy, wild and free.

So let's enjoy this funny show,
Growth and laughter in a row.
Nature's quirks bring joy anew,
In every sprout, life starts to cue.

The Serenade of Sunlight

Sunlight spills on the garden floor,
As flowers giggle, begging more.
Petals clap to the radiant beat,
A lovely tune from the sun's warm seat.

Bees hum in perfect harmony,
Singing praises to each flower, so free.
Wind joins in with a playful sway,
Dancing nature, lighting the day.

Every stalk sways with cheeky bliss,
Kissing the cloud with a playful twist.
While vegetable friends wink from below,
Sharing jokes only plants know.

The light fades, but laughter stays,
In this garden of sunny rays.
Each leaf and bloom, together they say,
Let's serenade life in a fun-filled way!

Cultivating Kindness

In the soil, kindness starts to grow,
Complementing friend with a gentle glow.
Weeds whisper softly, 'We're here to play!'
As gardens bloom and jokes come our way.

A sunflower offers a cup of sun,
While roses toss petals, just for fun.
Ferns hug the earth, oh what a sight,
Sharing warmth through day and night.

Every plant shares its little treat,
With roots intertwined, they can't be beat.
Laughter dances on the garden breeze,
As blossoms giggle beneath the trees.

Kindness wraps around like a vine,
Chasing shadows with love divine.
In this patch of earth, there's a sign,
Cultivating joy, oh how fine!

The Garden of Friendship

In a garden where laughter grows,
Flowers swap secrets in rows.
Bees blush at the jokes they hear,
Dandelions giggle, always near.

Toads sit on lilypads, quite proud,
Making puns that draw a crowd.
Worms tell tales of soil delight,
Under the moon, they party all night.

Sunflowers dance, reaching for cheer,
Tickling the wind with petals dear.
Veggies roll their eyes in fun,
As radishes race to the setting sun.

In this plot where friends convene,
Every leaf's a laughing machine.
Insects laugh and share their craft,
In the garden of friendship, joy's a laugh!

Echoing Roots of Trust

Beneath the soil where whispers play,
Roots exchange gossip every day.
Mushrooms giggle, sharing their spores,
While ivy climbs and knocks on doors.

Squirrels snicker at the oak's old tales,
Of storms and winds and passing gales.
The grasses sway in comedic grace,
While daisies wear a funny face.

The ferns shake hands, roots intertwining,
Building bonds of trust, so defining.
With every dig, a chuckle's found,
In the earth's embrace, where laughs abound.

So let's dig deep, and trust like trees,
In laughter's roots, we find our ease.
With every heartbeat, don't you see?
The echoing roots are kin to thee!

A Sprout's Soft Melody

A sprout in the garden hums a tune,
Softly singing to the golden moon.
With each gentle breeze, it sways and bends,
Composing symphonies for all its friends.

Petals sway and leaves tap, tap, tap,
As crickets join in for a nightcap.
Bumblebees buzz with a zesty beat,
Making music in the warm summer heat.

The daisies nod, keeping rhythm fine,
While the thyme sings of love, oh how divine!
In this concert of nature, laughter flows,
As the sprout's soft melody brightly glows.

So join the tune, don't be shy,
In the garden of mirth, let spirits fly.
With each note, we find our delight,
In a sprout's soft song under starlit night!

The Love Within Each Leaf

In every leaf, a giggle waits,
As saplings share, exchanging fates.
Green pals wave like they've lost their head,
Making sunshine smiles as they spread.

Butterflies flutter in a comical dance,
In a courtship that's purely by chance.
While petals flirt, the flowers all sway,
Creating a show in a bright bouquet.

Tree branches stretch as they high-five,
Cheering each other, feeling alive.
Roots tangle in a joyous embrace,
The love within each leaf finds its place.

So here's to the laughter, the fun we share,
In the leaf-filled realm, there's love everywhere.
In nature's hug, let's give a cheer,
For all the joy that blooms year after year!

The Silent Nurturer

In a pot sat a leafy friend,
Who'd wiggle and sway, never bend.
I talked to it daily, quite a delight,
Its green leaves would quiver, what a sight!

Watered it once, then I forgot,
Yet it stood still, not a single dot.
Ignoring my chores, all day I played,
With my shy plant, who never dismayed.

Every so often, I'd give it a wink,
Wondering what it's thinking, I'd blink.
Did it laugh when I spilled the can?
Or plot my demise? Oh, what a plan!

Chlorophyll dreams in the light's warm glow,
Supporting my antics, stealing the show.
With my silent nurturer, life's a jest,
Together we flourish, both truly blessed.

Petals of Connection

My buddy in green, with petals so bright,
Seems to giggle each day, oh what a sight!
A cactus that teases, spines all around,
It tickles my soul, laughter abound!

We share all our secrets, it knows all my quirks,
As I chat away, it gives playful smirks.
Through silly old jokes and stories of yore,
Together we giggle, like never before.

When I dance in the sunshine, it sways with delight,
With each silly twirl, we own the daylight.
"Keep your distance!" it seems to say,
But it's hard when it laughs all my worries away!

In this weird union, a bond will grow,
My leafy sidekick steals every show.
As friends in this chaos, come what may,
With petals a-flutter, we'll play all day.

Hope in Every Sprout

In the corner of the room, a sprout takes hold,
Whispers of laughter in its roots so bold.
Its leaves stand tall, with ambition and glee,
Playing hide and seek with the sun and me.

One little seed was all it took,
Now a comedic star from a simple book.
Sprouting up jokes, to brighten my day,
This green little genius loves to play!

A water dance happens with every rain,
Making puddles of joy, oh what a gain!
It jests with the breeze, a whimsical twist,
In every small leaf, a hope to persist.

As it stretches and grows, our laughter collides,
With roots as our bond, no need to hide.
In this quirky garden of friendship and fun,
Hope blooms in each sprout, as we share the sun.

A Friendship Grows

A small green friend sits on my desk,
Chatting away, I must confess.
With each passing day, our bond does grow,
Its leafy whispers never steal the show.

With every unkempt leaf and twisted vine,
It shares all my jokes, oh how they shine!
Compliments come in the shape of green,
"Don't worry," it says, "You're quite a scene!"

Whenever I fumble, it chuckles soft,
Its roots are the truths, where laughter can loft.
Each sprightly bloom tells a funny tale,
Of how we conquer life without fail.

So here's to my buddy, my wacky green mate,
With jokes in our hearts, we celebrate fate.
In this friendship of giggles, jokes, and puns,
Together we flourish, oh what fun runs!

Heartstrings in Bloom

In the garden, I did stumble,
Where petals laughed and flowers fumbled.
A daisy winked with a cheeky grin,
Said, "Come dance, let spring begin!"

I twirled with vines that liked to tease,
Their leafy fingers brushed my knees.
The roses giggled, blushing bright,
As bees buzzed by, a comical sight.

A sunflower bowed, wore a dapper hat,
While snapdragons snapped at a passing cat.
The whole lot roared, a floral jest,
In this garden, I felt quite blessed.

Laughter bloomed, it spread so wide,
With every petal, joy inside.
Who knew love could sprout this way?
Just ask the plants, they'll play all day!

A Garden's Tender Heart

In a patch where green thumbs excel,
The herbs all gathered for a swell.
Thyme said, "Hey, let's add a dash,
And make this garden really splash!"

The carrots chuckled in their patch,
"Oh look, the onions are in a batch!"
With garlic stinking up the space,
It turned into a funny race!

The daisies cheered from their soft beds,
"Let's create a crown for all our heads!"
They made a wreath of vibrant hues,
And danced away like plants with shoes.

Meanwhile, cacti poked fun at me,
"Hey buddy, mind the 'sting' – we're not free!"
With every giggle and playful shout,
This is what gardens are all about!

Seasons of Affection

Winter grinned with frosty breath,
While spring just laughed, "You're a mess!"
The snowflakes twirled, a dance so bright,
As blooms popped out, to winter's fright.

Summer swayed with sunlit cheer,
Said, "Come join, no room for fear!"
While autumn, with leaves like confetti,
Shouted, "Let's party, life's so meaty!"

They traded stories with chuckles loud,
Of storms and suns, they felt so proud.
Telling tales of growth and cheer,
Every season, a friend so dear.

So cheers to time, with laughter's blend,
In every phase, the fun won't end!
With plants to share in every shift,
Life's a garden, a wondrous gift!

Roots of Familiarity

The roots gathered in a tangled mess,
Said, "Let's bond, it's quite a success!"
Each vine embraced, growing so tight,
Yelling, "We'll dance into the night!"

A potato piped up, "Don't squash my fun!"
As the tomatoes rolled in a punny run.
"Watch out!" they cried, in playful jest,
While peas chuckled, feeling blessed.

The herbs brewed jokes in a pot so sweet,
"Mix it up, this can't be beat!"
Like thyme and basil made a pair,
Spicing the air with love to spare.

With roots so deep, their message clear,
"We stick together, that's our cheer!"
In this garden, full of glee,
The best of friends, just wait and see!

In Blooming Harmony

In a pot by the window, I found a sprout,
It danced in the sunlight, it twisted about.
With leaves like confetti, it threw quite a show,
I laughed till I cried, oh, it steals the glow.

The neighbors all gossip, they think it's too bold,
To chat with my plant, or so I am told.
But who needs a friend when you've got a sweet herb?
My basil sings love songs, oh, it's quite the verb!

We share all our secrets, the mint, it does tease,
While daisies listen closely, they sway in the breeze.
I promised them vodka, just one tiny sip,
But they clucked in protest, "We're full of good quip!"

With petals in laughter, the garden's alive,
My leafy companions, they help me survive.
We giggle at pigeons, and chatter with bees,
In this funny little world, no worries, just leaves!

Foliage of Fondness

A cactus once whispered, 'Don't poke at my pride,'
But I laughed as I trimmed back its thorns, well supplied.
It shot me a look that could wither a star,
Yet I grinned, for I knew it was all just bizarre.

Oh, lavender lies low, with aromas so bold,
It dreams of grand parties, champagne made of gold.
"Invite all the bees!" it buzzed with delight,
But those critters are picky; they party all night!

The ferns form a circle, with gossip to share,
While vines climb the walls, they swoon with flair.
"Let's throw a wild rave, with roots in the ground!"
So I grooved with my greenery, happiness found!

And when day turns to night, with stars shining bright,
I ponder the laughter, the green things in sight.
I hug all my buddies, in this garden of glee,
For life is a funny, leafy jamboree!

Whispers of Green

A petunia once told me, 'Life is a jest,'
With petals a-winking, it laughed with the best.
I asked, 'What's the trick?' with a grin on my face,
It said, 'Just keep growing — it's all a race!'

The orchids wore bow ties, so dapper and spry,
Sipping dew from the morn, they looked quite sly.
"More sun, less drama!" they shouted with glee,
As I joined in their revels, with snacks from the tea!

The roses took selfies, "Say cheese!" they all cheered,
But thorns popped the balloon when they felt quite weird.

"It's photosynthesis, not a viral spree!"
Yet laughter erupted, oh, how we did spree!

In this little jungle, where whimsy is king,
I bask in the jokes that my greenery brings.
With each silly moment, I giggle and beam,
For plants with a sense of humor, what a dream!

Embrace of the Vines

Tangled in laughter, the vines spun around,
Each twist was a story, the wildness unbound.
"I'm not just a plant; I'm a friend in disguise,"
Said the ivy, winking with green, gleeful eyes.

The garden weeps joy, with colors so bright,
As daisies do the cha-cha under moonlight.
"Join us, dear human! We'll have a grand time!"
I laughed as they joked, with rhythm and rhyme.

With petals a-flutter, they hold on so tight,
"Dance with the daisies, we'll party all night!"
And when morning breaks, oh, the fun we have spun,
In this leafy embrace, every day's just begun!

So here's to the foliage, the whims that we chase,
With laughter as fertilizer, we find our own space.
A garden of giggles, where humor entwines,
In this silly little world, forever are vines!

Living Memories in the Garden

I swear I saw a flower dance,
With petals flapping in a trance.
It winked at me, oh what a sight,
A true delight in morning light.

The carrots sang a silly tune,
While broccoli played on a wooden spoon.
Lettuce giggled, swayed in glee,
"Come join our party, just you and me!"

A radish told a joke, so bright,
"Told my friends I'd outgrow the height!"
Then sprouted up, just a bit too tall,
And bumped its head against the wall.

In this garden, laughter grows,
With every leaf, a tale that flows.
Join the fun, come peek and see,
What silly secrets bloom, just free!

The Promise Made in Petals

A daisy swore it'd never wilt,
Promised love, no matter how built.
But every breeze would make it sway,
And whisper jokes to brighten the day.

The roses formed a comedy troupe,
With thorns that poked, but hearts that loop.
They bloomed in colors loud and proud,
Buggin' the bees who danced, so loud.

"Hey! What's green and sings?" they joked,
"A celery!" The garden choked.
Laughter echoed 'round the patch,
With every jest, a loving match.

In every petal, fun was sown,
Promises made, together grown.
With quirks and quirks, they'd never part,
A garden bursting with funny heart!

Symbiotic Sentiments

The fungi winked, "I'm your best mate!"
While roots wrapped tight in friendship state.
"Let's share some water, I'll lend you cheer,
With me, you'll never shed a tear!"

A sunflower leaned with a goofy grin,
"Can I be the tallest? Let the fun begin!"
Buds laughed hard, sharing their delight,
In the warmth of the golden sunlight.

The bees buzzed in with stories galore,
"Who stole my nectar? Oh, I want more!"
The flowers all chimed, "It's a bee-sy life,
One poor mistake leads to buzz and strife!"

In this patch, each twirl and twist,
Grows the friendship we can't resist.
With just a laugh, our bonds grow tight,
In nature's dance, what a funny sight!

Gardens of Unspoken Bonds

In quiet spots where veggies grow,
A secret language starts to flow.
Tomatoes wink, green beans tease,
Together they sway in the playful breeze.

A sunflower whispered to a vine,
"Let's intertwine and feel divine!"
With every twist, their friendship bloomed,
In this garden, laughter loomed.

The carrots giggle, "Let's dress for spring!"
With hats of dirt, in every fling.
Radishes chuckle, "What's in a name?"
"We're all just roots playing a game!"

Unspoken bonds in sunlit land,
With every sprout, a helping hand.
So take a peek, join the fun,
In our garden, we're never done!

Heartbeats in the Garden

In my garden, flowers giggle,
They dance around, not shy a wiggle.
Bees buzzing with a silly hum,
Even the weeds join in the fun.

Sunshine paints the petals bright,
While worms are wiggling with delight.
A rainbow sneezed—a splash of hue,
Oh, what a sight the blooms can do!

The daisies whisper jokes of old,
While tulips strut, all proud and bold.
The roses blush, they hear the news,
Of how the violets share their shoes.

And when the evening shadows creep,
The crickets join the laughter deep.
In the garden, mirth has grown,
A world where no one feels alone.

The Touch of Nature's Hand

In the woods, a leaf once chuckled,
As a squirrel nearby just buckled.
With acorns falling like confetti,
The laughter spread, it seemed so petty.

A stream that flows with giggles too,
Rides over rocks where bubbles brew.
The trees sway gently, high and low,
As if they're putting on a show.

Flowers sprout, with faces wide,
They joke about a leafy ride.
A butterfly lands with grace to laugh,
Sharing secrets in the sun's warm bath.

In this haven of leafy cheer,
EveryVisitor meets a friend here.
A world wrapped in green's gentle hand,
Forever blessed in nature's band.

A Journey Through Green

Took a stroll through a leafy maze,
Where trees dressed up in bright green bays.
The ferns waved like they knew my name,
And each flower blushed, a blooming fame.

A snail shared tales of its long plight,
How it creeps and dreams at night.
The grass tickled my toes so free,
In this world, joy is the key!

Over hills of daisies I pranced,
While mischievous insects sweetly danced.
A ladybug led the joyful parade,
In nature's heart, memories are made.

As I journeyed through fields so wide,
Everywhere, the green folks smiled wide.
Life's a comedy in shades of hue,
Come join the mirth, there's room for you!

Life's Floral Embrace

In a patch where daisies bloom,
A bumblebee walks with much to groom.
Petal friends gossip from up high,
While blades of grass wave bye-bye.

The sun dips low, the shadows play,
Cacti do the cha-cha all day.
A lavender winked, a marigold grinned,
In their floral hug, all woes rescind.

Pansies in silly hats trot about,
While busy ants march, no doubt.
Each twig and sprout shares a laugh,
Creating joy in nature's half.

With roots entwined in laughter tight,
They spread warmth through the cool of night.
In their colorful, chaotic embrace,
I've found a home, a funny place.

Growing Together

In the garden, we share a space,
You giggle at my dirty face.
With roots intertwined, a playful team,
We dance with joy, or so it seems.

Sunshine kisses our leafy hair,
While ants march by without a care.
We sway with laughter, oh what a sight,
In this silly green world, everything's right.

I water you, you drink with glee,
You whisper secrets, just to me.
Though always hungry for some light,
You say, 'Hold on, I'm not a bite!'

Every day is a brand new game,
Growing close, we're never the same.
Together we bloom, all shades and hues,
Nature's jesters, with nothing to lose.

Nature's Affectionate Touch

With a gentle breeze, you tickle my leaves,
Each day we play as sunlight weaves.
You laugh as raindrops make me sway,
'Time to shower!' I shout, come what may.

Your roots beneath, they tickle mine,
In this quirky dance, our hearts align.
I share my soil, you share your shade,
In this crazy bond, memories are made.

When pests parade, we shout with glee,
'Come and get us, if you dare!', says me.
We joke about growing taller than the moon,
Plant life is funny, just like a cartoon!

So here's to us, the greenest pair,
With blossoms bright and fragrant air.
Together we laugh, let nature adore,
With each silly moment, we both want more.

The Verdant Bond

You and I, we sprout and stretch,
With every laugh, we truly mesh.
I hear you chuckle when breezes come,
Oh what joy, we're never glum!

A little sun and a dash of rain,
We bounce back, never complain.
You're my buddy, through thick and thin,
With you, my roots, I know I'll win.

In this wild garden, we find our cheer,
Waving at bugs that draw near.
Together we thrive, twist, and tease,
Nature's own jesters, putting minds at ease.

So here's to fun in our leafy embrace,
Growing together, finding our space.
With laughter and love, we face the day,
In this veggie world, we play and sway!

A Symphony of Leaves

In the forest, we make quite the show,
Rustling together, like a giggling duo.
You hum a tune, I sway to the beat,
Underneath the sun, we dance, oh so sweet.

With every gust, our laughter flies,
Spreading seeds of joy to the skies.
You nudge me close, whispering low,
'Let's trick the bees and steal the show!'

Our branches twist in a silly embrace,
While squirrels laugh and join the race.
We'll host a party, with fungi and moss,
In this grand symphony, we'll never be lost.

Let's paint the world in shades of fun,
From dawn's first light to the setting sun.
With nature's rhythm, we'll keep it bright,
A green concerto, dancing in delight.

Blooming Affection

In the corner, something grew,
With petals bright, not quite the hue.
It whispered secrets of the sun,
And claimed my heart—oh, what a pun!

With watering can, mischievous plot,
To see how much love could be bought.
I sang to it with silly cheer,
Where flowers laughed, and I shed a tear.

The neighbors peeked, in pure delight,
As I danced with my plant each night.
Its leaves would shimmy, twist, and sway,
I thought it loved my clumsy way!

Oh, how it bloomed, a sight to see,
With tiny bugs as company.
Love in the garden, who would have guessed?
A blooming heart, it truly blessed!

Roots of Devotion

In shadows deep, where sunlight strays,
A quirky stalk began to gaze.
It dug its roots in loyalty,
And claimed my heart so forcefully!

I'd chat sweet nonsense, day and night,
While pretending it could take flight.
Each leaf would nod, or so it seemed,
Oh, how I marveled, truly dreamed!

I wore a smile, it bloomed with pride,
Together we'd go for a joyride.
The neighbors laughed and joined the show,
This love affair, we'd surely grow!

With dirt beneath and fun above,
What a delightful kind of love!
Roots so entwined, I can't complain,
In my garden, joy's not vain!

The Green Caress

In the sunny spot of my abode,
There lived a sprout, in green bestowed.
It waved at me with gentle grace,
In its bright leaves, I found my place.

With every sip of water shared,
I felt a bond that truly bared.
I'd tickle stems; it laughed with glee,
A friendship forged, just it and me!

We'd sway together in the breeze,
As I'd tell jokes, we'd both feel pleased.
It grew so wild, our silly fun,
A merry duo, 'neath the sun!

And as it flourished, so did my grin,
With every inch, I felt the win.
A green caress, too bright to miss,
In the garden of laughter, we shared bliss!

A Love Blooms in Soil

Beneath my feet, a mystery brews,
With every dig, the garden woos.
A tiny sprout with dreams on high,
I spoke to it, and it wouldn't lie!

We made a pact, a fun charade,
In sun and shade, our joys displayed.
It told me tales of roots and rain,
With every whisper, I felt no pain.

Its petals fan a lovely smile,
It danced around, oh what a style!
I'd twirl in joy, as if to say,
Our love is bright, let's seize the day!

So here's to blooms, beneath the sun,
With every bud, it's more than fun.
In soil of laughter, we both rejoice,
A love that's silly, and has a voice!

Cultivating Compassion

In a pot so small, my friend did grow,
With leaves that tickle, when breezes blow.
A little sprout, with eyes so wide,
It winked at me, full of pride.

I watered it well, with laughter and glee,
It danced on the sill, so merry and free.
It told me jokes, in whispers and sighs,
Promising sunshine, beneath cloudy skies.

When I felt blue, it donned a clown hat,
With petals like trousers, imagine that!
Its roots would wiggle, in pure delight,
As I shared my secrets, late in the night.

Together we thrived, like peas in a pod,
A quirky duo, oh how we trod.
With giggles and grins, we bloomed side by side,
In this wacky garden, where love can't hide.

The Language of Leaves

The leaves would chatter, like gossiping friends,
Spreading wild rumors, as the day ends.
They'd rustle and giggle, in breezy delight,
As I tried to listen, with all of my might.

Each morning, they'd wear a new shade of green,
A fashion statement, unlike any seen.
Dancing like pop stars, in sunlight's embrace,
With little leaf hands, they'd wave in the space.

They taught me to smile, with roots down below,
That joy is contagious, like a plant's playful show.
Bright buds sharing secrets, without any words,
A humorous chat between flowers and birds.

As seasons shifted, so did their style,
From vibrant to shy, but always with a smile.
Their laughter echoed, on every sweet breeze,
The language of leaves brought me to my knees.

An Arbor of Affection

Underneath the boughs, a canopy grand,
A comical squirrel, in a top hat, did stand.
He tipped it with flair, and danced on a limb,
As I clapped along, my laughter not dim.

The branches would chuckle, whispering sweet jests,
Promising moments of ample digests.
When I sat near, they'd rustle with glee,
An arbor of laughter, just waiting for me.

Each tree had a tale, with knots as the lines,
Of mischief and mayhem, of sun-drenched designs.
Together we'd giggle, as clouds rolled on by,
In this wild forest, where silliness flies.

The roots lay a dance floor, beneath the bright moon,
With shadows for partners, we'd sway to a tune.
In the shade of affection, we'd all come to play,
A humorous gathering, brightening the day.

Fields of Connection

In fields of green, where the daisies laugh,
A tangle of stems, composing a staff.
They played silly songs, with bees as the choir,
Planting seeds of joy, that would never tire.

With sunlight as ketchup, and moonlight as fries,
The flowers had tastes, oh what a surprise!
They held a feast, on petals so bright,
Inviting all critters, to join in the night.

Each blade of grass shared a giggle or two,
While worms wore bow ties, gracing their view.
Those fields were alive, with laughter and cheer,
To nurture each moment, with friendship so dear.

A picnic of colors, where blooms came to play,
They'd tell funny stories, all night and all day.
In this patch of mirth, love boldly would sprout,
In fields of connection, there's never a doubt.

The Heartfelt Harvest

In a garden bright and green,
A sprout danced with glee,
It wiggled and it jiggled,
And said, "Look at me!"

A carrot wore a silly hat,
Turnips joined the parade,
They joked about the weather,
And the sunlight they've made.

In pots of clay, they giggle,
As raindrops plop and plink,
Their roots in secret whispers,
Share secrets with a wink!

So here's to each green buddy,
With leaves that dance and sway,
The harvest brings us laughter,
In nature's funny way.

Lush Sentiments

In a patch of vibrant blooms,
A tulip wore a crown,
Declaring with a flourish,
"I'm the best around!"

A daisy rolled its petals,
And laughed without a care,
While shrubs pulled off their branches,
To join the revelry there.

With chatter among the roots,
And squirrels who like to dance,
The flowers shared their stories,
In nature's smirking prance.

So let us raise a watering can,
To those who bring us cheer,
In this garden of antics,
Where love grows year by year.

The Love Within the Soil

Deep in the dirt, a worm declared,
"This ground's a cozy bed!"
With squiggly glee, he told his friends,
"We'll nestle here instead!"

A beet sprouting with sassiness,
Said, "I'm the sweetest root!"
While radishes made funny faces,
And danced around in boots.

Each leaf with a cheeky shimmer,
Brought laughter to the air,
As beetles rolled in tumbleweeds,
Creating quite a flair!

So here's to dirt and friendships,
That grow beneath the sun,
In the wonder of the soil,
Where giggles are a ton.

Echoes of Nature's Care

In whispers soft, the daisies spoke,
"That bee just stole our show!"
With petals quivering in delight,
They giggled as they grow.

A sunflower stretched its neck up high,
And winked at passing clouds,
"I'm brighter than your curtain,
And prouder than your crowds!"

The breeze played tag with leafy friends,
While shadows danced around,
Nature's laughter echoed wide,
In this enchanted ground.

So let us cherish all the fun,
That blossoms in the air,
For in every living moment,
Is laughter everywhere.

Serenade of the Sunlit Sanctuary

In a sunny spot, so merry and bright,
I found a friend, oh what a sight!
With leaves that danced, and cheered me on,
We laughed together, from dusk till dawn.

Got a little pot, on a windowsill,
My leafy mate, with dreams to fulfill.
It whispered jokes, oh what a tease,
Made me giggle, with such ease.

The sun would shine, they'd sway with glee,
I'd sing to them, under the tree.
In our little world, so full of cheer,
A secret life, we held so dear.

With soil and sunshine, we made quite a pair,
A comedy duo, without a care.
When asked "How's your plant?" I'd proudly chime,
"We're thriving, my friend, one leaf at a time!"

Blossoms of Care

In a garden plot, where giggles bloom,
My green companion spread joy like a loom.
With petals like smiles, so funny and bright,
Together we bask in warm morning light.

Watering woes, did I ever relate?
I splashed a bit too much—what a fate!
My silly buddy, with roots so deep,
Gave me a wink, as if to keep.

Every morning, we'd share a joke,
They'd bud and bloom, like laughter they spoke.
In every sprout, a tale to tell,
Of friendships found, I knew them well.

With a little sun and a sprinkle of cheer,
Every visit to my garden, brings a sneer.
"Do you think plants care?" hey, that's absurd!
But drop some crumbs, and watch the word!

Echoes of Sacred Roots

Beneath the surface, their giggles abound,
Secrets in dirt, where joy can be found.
Roots intertwined, like stories we share,
With whispers of love, in the cool morning air.

Each leaf a joke, each bud a jest,
My plant's a comedian, simply the best!
They twist and turn, with a humorous flair,
In the dance of growth, I find them rare.

"Be careful!" I caution, "you might just grow tall!"
"Like a clumsy giraffe," they'd chuckle, enthralled.
And so we'd laugh, day in, day out,
This friend of mine, without a doubt.

From roots to tops, we're a funny pair,
In this silly garden, without a care.
As petals unfurl, our giggles resound,
In the echoes of joy, we both have found.

When Green Meets Heart

One day I woke, to a leafy surprise,
A green little buddy, with curious eyes.
"Hey there!" I greeted, "What do you need?"
"Some sunshine and laughs, please take heed!"

With a tap on the pot, I started the show,
Leaves would shimmy, a fun little flow.
We'd chat about weather, and how it's a bummer,
When rain falls down, it's a big ol' slumber.

I told them my dreams, they nodded along,
Sprouted a smile, in perfect song.
With a twist and a turn, they'd poke out a leaf,
"Pack the jokes, my friend — let's be brief!"

Together we'd giggle, a delightful team,
In this green little world, we'd scheme and dream.
So here's to the friend that brings joy to my day,
In laughter and blooms, they'll always stay!

Songs from the Greenhouse

In shady corners, secrets bloom,
With pots and pans, we dig up gloom.
A cactus sings in scratchy tones,
While herbs just laugh, creating drones.

The ivy twirls, a dance so slick,
The sunflowers can't help but click.
We gather round, no need for wine,
A grower's party, oh so fine!

With soil in one hand, tea in the other,
We toast to roots, like sister and brother.
The daisies giggle, petals all a-quiver,
In this greenhouse, our hearts deliver.

So cheers to greens, their quirky fun,
Life's a garden, never done!
With friends and pots, we laugh out loud,
To nature's quirks, we're ever proud.

Cradled in Chlorophyll

In jungles thick, where laughter grows,
I met a fern, and it knows.
A potbelly cactus, quite the tease,
Joking around, it's sure to please.

The leaves are whispering, jokes on repeat,
The petals with giggles, no need for a seat.
A flower sneezed, oh what a sight!
The pollen floated, a funny flight!

Around the roots where we do play,
A snail slips by, making his way.
"Slow down, buddy, you'll miss the show!"
He winked and smiled, "Not to worry, though!"

In this chlorophyll cradle, life's a jest,
Each sprout's a charmer, each leaf's a guest.
We chat with the daisies, what tales do unearth,
In the garden, we create our mirth!

The Tender Shoot

A sprout looked up at skies so high,
"Why can't we dance? Let's give it a try!"
With wiggles and giggles, they swayed in the breeze,
Attracting the bees who buzz with ease.

The marigold winked, "Give it a spin,
Let's shake up this garden, let the fun begin!"
With roots in the dirt and dreams in the air,
These little green stars make quite the pair.

A shy little seed, he watched from afar,
"Can I join in? I'm no rock star!"
"Of course!" said the others, "We love you brave!"
In the soil of laughter, all were saved.

At sunset they gathered, each one with a tale,
Of sunshine and raindrops, and a friendly snail.
With every sprout, the joy did multiply,
In their funny garden, they reached for the sky!

Whispers from the Soil

Below the surface, where giggles hide,
The worms exchange rumors, side by side.
"Did you hear? The daisies went out of style!"
"Not in my book, they're always worth a smile!"

The dirt grumbles softly, a wise old sage,
"Life's too short to be stuck in a cage."
With roots intertwining, they plot and they scheme,
Creating a world that flows like a dream.

The radishes mock with their round little hats,
While carrots chat gossip; oh, what of the cats?
"Did you see that squirrel? Quite a brave little chap,
He tried to steal our seeds and had quite a mishap!"

So here in the muck, wit takes its place,
In green-coated laughter, life finds its grace.
With whispers of joy that weaves through the ground,
The heart of the garden forever unbound!

Sentinels of Sunshine

In the garden, green guards sway,
Watching me stumble, day by day.
With leaves that whisper, smiles they share,
I trip on roots; they just don't care.

They giggle under the golden rays,
Taking bets on my clumsy ways.
Every bloom seems to wink at me,
As I waddle like a bumblebee.

Their branches wave; it's quite a show,
I feel the warmth of cheer, you know.
With petals dancing, oh what a sight,
Even weeds laugh at my lack of might.

So here's to my leafy friends so tall,
Together we stumble, we laugh, we crawl.
Through twirls of wind, we celebrate,
Nature's jesters, and we're feeling great!

Nature's Tender Embrace

In the wild, where oddities thrive,
A tree hugs me, oh how I jive!
With arms so wide, it won't let go,
While I wiggle like I'm in a show.

The daisies cheer as I twirl around,
Bouncing off mushrooms, I hit the ground.
A chorus of laughter fills the air,
As butterflies tease my wild hair.

The grass softy tickles my toes,
I sway and giggle; oh, how time flows.
With every leaf falling in play,
Nature laughs at my silly display.

Underneath the sun's warm grin,
Nature and I share this goofy spin.
Holding hands with a tree divine,
In this embrace, life feels just fine!

Portrait of a Petal

There's a rosy flower with a big face,
"It's time to shine!" it says with grace.
I pose beside it, striking a chord,
Its antics leave me utterly floored.

"Hold still now!" the flower demands,
While the wind makes silly hands.
Petals giggle, color me bright,
As bees hum tunes of sheer delight.

With brushes of pollen, they paint a scene,
A canvas of chaos, so bright and green.
Though I try to stay poised and fair,
My laughter spills out like the fresh air.

Snapshot in petals, captured in fun,
A vibrant portrait beneath the sun.
Together we burst, with joy in each hue,
Nature's art is nothing but true!

Vines of Connection

With vines that giggle, weaving so high,
They tie me up, oh my oh my!
In a twirl of green, I find my way,
Tripping over roots in a playful display.

"Oooh, look at you!" the tendrils tease,
As I tumble over and scrape my knees.
Each leaf a witness to my clumsy fall,
Yet their laughter rings; they love it all.

Tangled in friendships, a leafy embrace,
Vines and I spin in this crazy race.
Every twist brings a hearty cheer,
"Try again!" they whisper, "No need to fear!"

In this garden, with camaraderie bright,
I dance with the vines; they hold me tight.
Together we grow, with laughter in tow,
In this vine-filled joy, we always glow!

www.ingramcontent.com/pod-product-compliance
Lightning Source LLC
Chambersburg PA
CBHW070326120526
44590CB00017B/2823